SECOND EDITION

GUIDE TO
Public Housing
Conversions under
RAD

Amy M. McClain and Courtney E. Hunter

ABA

AMERICAN**BAR**ASSOCIATION

Forum on Affordable
Housing and Community
Development

29 28 27 26 25   5 4 3 2 1

Library of Congress Cataloging-in-Publication Data

Names: McClain, Amy M. author | Hunter, Courtney E author | American Bar Association. Forum on Affordable Housing and Community Development Law issuing body
Title: Guide to public housing conversions under HUD's rental assistance demonstration program / Amy M McClain and Courtney E Hunter.
Other titles: Beginner's guide to public housing conversion under RAD
Description: Second edition. | Chicago : Forum on Affordable Housing, American Bar Association, 2026. | Includes bibliographical references and index. | Summary: "This Guide details public housing conversions under the First Component, but it does not cover the conversion of affordable units in privately-owned properties that receive assistance under legacy subsidy programs under the Second Component"— Provided by publisher.
Identifiers: LCCN 2025044229 | ISBN 9781639057061 paperback | ISBN 9781639057078 epub
Subjects: LCSH: United States. Department of Housing and Urban Development | Public housing—Law and legislation—United States | Public housing—Finance—Law and legislation—United States | Federal aid to housing—United States | Housing rehabilitation—Law and legislation—United States | Rent subsidies—Law and legislation—United States | Housing subsidies—Law and legislation—United States
Classification: LCC KF5729 .M33 2026
LC record available at https://lccn.loc.gov/2025044229

ISBN 978-1-63905-
Discounts are available for books ordered in bulk. Special consideration is given to state bars, CLE programs, and other bar-related organizations. Inquire at Book Publishing, ABA Publishing, American Bar Association, 321 N. Clark Street, Chicago, Illinois 60654-7598.

www.shopABA.org

Contents

1 Program Overview   1

2 RAD Feasibility Analysis   5

3 Resident Engagement   9

4 Application Submission   13

5 Statutory and Regulatory Waivers and Considerations   19

6 Resident Protections   27

7 Relocation   31

8 CHAP Award and Pre-Financing Plan Activities   41

9 Financing Plan   43

10 RAD Conversion Commitment and Closing Process   45

11 Post-Conversion Processing   47

12 RAD/Section 18 Blend   49

13 Restore–Rebuild   53

Conclusion   57

About the Authors   59

Index   61

Program Overview 1

The U.S. Department of Housing and Urban Development (HUD) initiated the Rental Assistance Demonstration (RAD) as a tool for preserving affordable housing and addressing the growing backlog of capital improvement needs for public housing and HUD-subsidized projects across the nation. RAD seeks to preserve at-risk affordable housing by converting the federal rental subsidy provided by the public housing program (First Component) or legacy subsidy programs (Second Component) to the Section 8 program, using either project-based rental assistance (PBRA) or project-based vouchers (PBV).

Precursors to RAD, including the Transforming Rental Assistance initiative proposed by HUD to Congress as part of the fiscal year (FY) 2011 federal budget process, raised concerns among lawmakers regarding the need for budget neutrality, resident protections, and a means of measuring the impact of any transformation effort. Once these concerns were addressed, Congress approved RAD through the Consolidated and Further Continuing Appropriations Act of 2012 (2012 Appropriations Act).[1]

This Guide details public housing conversions under the First Component, but it does not cover the conversion of affordable units in privately owned properties that receive assistance under legacy subsidy programs under the Second Component.

---

1 The Consolidated and Further Continuing Appropriations Act of 2012, Pub. L. No. 112–55 (adopted Nov. 18, 2011).

Under RAD's First Component, public housing agencies (PHA) convert Section 9 rental assistance from public housing to long-term, project-based Section 8 rental assistance by way of Housing Assistance Payments (HAP) contracts under the U.S. Housing Act of 1937, as amended (Housing Act). The owner of a RAD-converted project can leverage the Section 8 assistance provided by the new HAP contract against private and public debt and equity in order to generate the capital needed to repair or replace rental units. Once within the Section 8 framework, the RAD units function more like private housing with greater access to financing resources and fewer regulatory limitations.

Thus far, Congress has not appropriated any additional federal funds to support public housing properties converting under the RAD program. Instead, HUD must repurpose existing public housing funding streams, namely, public housing Operating Funds and public housing Capital Funds, to finance the new HAP contracts post-conversion.[2] Unfortunately, because public housing funding levels are limited, some public housing properties cannot support the costs of necessary redevelopment work with HAP contract rents at the current public housing funding levels.[3]

To further limit the demonstration's fiscal impact, the new HAP contracts executed in connection with RAD conversions only allow for rents to be adjusted by an operating cost adjustment factor (OCAF) instead of allowing the rents to be adjusted to reflect fair market rents in the area, which may exceed the OCAF.[4]

PHAs interested in RAD may submit applications for a specific project (using the HUD form of RAD application) or a portfolio of projects. If the PHA applies for a portfolio award, HUD will reserve authority under the

---

2 *Id.* at [10].

3 *See* U.S. Dep't of Hous. & Urb. Dev., FY 2020 Budget in Brief 6–8, https://archives.hud.gov/budget/fy20/2020CJ-PHOperatingFund.pdf; U.S. Dep't of Hous. & Urb. Dev., FY 2021 Budget in Brief 12, https://archives.hud.gov/budget/fy21/BudgetinBrief_2020-02_06_Online.pdf.

4 2012 Appropriations Act, as amended by Consolidated Appropriations Act, 2014 (P.L. 113–76); Consolidated and Further Continuing Appropriations Act, 2015 (P.L. 113–235); Consolidated Appropriations Act, 2016 (P.L. 114–113) (FY 2016 Act); Consolidated Appropriations Act, 2017 (P.L. 115–31); Consolidated Appropriations Act, 2018 (P.L. 115–141) (FY 2018 Act); and Consolidated Appropriations Act, 2024 (P.L. 118–42) (FY 2024 Act) (collectively, the RAD Statute).

RAD Unit Cap (as such term is defined later) for the number of units covered by the award, and the PHA will be required to submit a RAD application for each individual project.

Following its review and approval of the RAD application, HUD will issue a Commitment to Enter into a Housing Assistance Payment (CHAP), after which the PHA will prepare and submit a Financing Plan for HUD to approve.

After HUD approval of the Financing Plan, HUD will issue a RAD Conversion Commitment (RCC), after which the PHA will prepare and submit the closing document submission in accordance with the RAD closing checklist for HUD's review. Once HUD is satisfied with the draft closing documents, the conversion can occur.

At conversion, the former public housing property will be (1) removed from the public housing program; (2) released from the HUD Declaration of Trust or Declaration of Restrictive Covenants, as applicable; (3) subject to a RAD Use Agreement; and (4) receiving subsidy pursuant to a long-term HAP contract.

The former public housing property is known as the Converting Project; the property that receives subsidy pursuant to the RAD HAP contract is known as the Covered Project.

Originally, the program only permitted conversions for up to 60,000 units, but the FY 2018 Appropriations Act[5] increased the cap on program conversions to up to 455,000 public housing units (as may be increased, the RAD Unit Cap). As of July 2025, 184,805 units have converted through the program, 64,217 units are actively moving through the conversion process, 134,030 units are in the application process, and 71,948 unit slots are available for conversion out of the 455,000 unit cap.[6]

RAD currently has a program sunset date of September 30, 2029 (Program Sunset Date),[7] but industry leaders are hopeful that the Program

---

5 FY 2018 Act.

6 RAD Resource Desk, https://www.radresource.net/pha_data2020.cfm (last visited Aug. 16, 2025).

7 FY 2024 Act.

Sunset Date and the RAD Unit Cap will be extended or even eliminated in future legislation.

RAD remains a demonstration program. Consequently, HUD has not yet developed new regulations to govern the program. Instead, the program is governed by statute and notice, and it continues to evolve. This Guide seeks to provide an overview of the rules and procedures that are currently in place in relation to the conversion of public housing units to Section 8 assistance. We will also strive to provide an update to the Guide as needed, given the changing nature of the program. However, readers should also consult the latest RAD implementation notice[8] (RAD Notice) for the most current program requirements.

---

8 As of the publication date of this Guide, the current RAD implementation notice is Rental Assistance Demonstration—Final Implementation, Revision 4, H-2019-09 PIH-2019-23 (HA) (as supplemented, REV-4 Notice). REV-4 Notice replaces PIH Notice 2018-22, issued on December 11, 2018. PIH Notice 2018-22 was preceded by PIH Notice 2018-11 issued on July 2, 2018. The initial notice, PIH Notice 2012-32, was issued on July 26, 2012. Four revisions implementing modifications and corrections to the PIH Notice 2012-32 were issued on July 2, 2013; Feb. 6, 2014; June 15, 2015; and Jan.12, 2017. PIH Notice 2012-32 was preceded by PIH Notice 2012-18, issued on March 8, 2012.

RAD Feasibility Analysis 2

The RAD application requires the submission of a conversion plan and a Financing Plan that HUD will review to assess the long-term physical and financial feasibility of a potential RAD project. The RAD application requires the PHA to provide particular project details to enable HUD to confirm whether the potential project meets certain eligibility thresholds.

HUD established an online portal known as the RAD Resource Desk,[1] which provides a variety of tools intended to assist PHAs and their development partners with the RAD planning process.

As part of the RAD application, HUD expects PHAs to set an overall schedule for conversion, identify potential lenders and investors, prepare for the Capital Needs Assessment (CNA) to be conducted once the CHAP is issued, and develop a plan for addressing existing debt secured by the property and/or public housing subsidies proposed for RAD conversion.

HUD also encourages PHAs to determine as part of the initial assessment whether the RAD conversion will use PBV or PBRA

---

11   www.radresource.net.

assistance. This assessment may consider the following elements when comparing the two types of assistance:

Element	PBV	PBRA
Contract Term	15–20 years.	20 years.
Mandatory Contract Renewal	Upon contract expiration, administering PHA must offer, and project owner must accept, a contract renewal.	Upon contract expiration, HUD Secretary or contract administrator must offer, and project owner must accept, a contract renewal.
Administrator	PHA with existing Housing Choice Voucher program.	HUD (for initial RAD conversions) or other HUD-approved contract administrator.
Contract Rents	Lower of: • Current public housing funding (Operating Funds and Capital Funds); • 110% of fair market rent (FMR) (minus utility allowance); or • reasonable rent.	Lower of: • Current public housing funding (Operating Funds and Capital Funds); or • 120% of FMR (minus utility allowance).
Rent Adjustments	• OCAF up to reasonable rent and subject to appropriations. • Note that Section 8(o)(13)(I) of the Housing Act and 24 C.F.R. §§ 983.301 and 983.302 are not applicable.	• OCAF subject to appropriations. • Note that Section 8(c)(2) of the Housing Act and 24 C.F.R. § 880.609 are not applicable.
Fees to PHA	• Asset management fee may be paid to the PHA either as a "must pay" operating expense or from cash flow; • for the remainder of the calendar year following conversion, the PHA will not receive any administrative fees under the HAP; and • such fees may be paid after the remainder of the first calendar year has expired.	• Asset management fee may be paid only from cash flow.

Element	PBV	PBRA
Resident Choice-Mobility	• Resident is eligible for a tenant-based Housing Choice Voucher (TBV) after one (1) year of residency, using the first available TBV in accordance with Section 8(o)(13)(E) of the U.S. Housing Act of 1937; and • the Choice-Mobility requirement cannot be waived.	• Resident is eligible for a TBV upon the later of (1) 24 months from the HAP effective date; or (2) 24 months after the resident's move-in date. • The PHA providing the TBV need not provide more than one-third of its turnover vouchers to the residents of covered RAD PBRA projects. • On a project basis, the PHA may limit Choice-Mobility moves to no more than 15% of the PBRA-assisted units within the project.
Cap on Number of Assisted Units	No cap on the number of units that may receive RAD PBV assistance in the project, as permitted by a HUD waiver of Section 8(o)(13)(D) and the Housing Opportunity Through Modernization Act of 2016, as well as related provisions of 24 C.F.R. §§ 983.56, 983.257(b), 983.262(a) and (d).	• No cap. • PBRA projects converted under RAD are treated as Pre-1981 Act projects under Section 16(c) of the U.S. Housing Act of 1937 and thus may rent up to 25% of the units to households with incomes "other than very low-income" (i.e., to households with incomes above 50% and at or below 80% of area median income).
Environmental Review	An environmental review under 24 C.F.R. Part 50 must be completed and submitted no later than the Financing Plan.	An environmental review under 24 C.F.R. Part 50 must be completed and submitted no later than the Financing Plan.

Resident Engagement

3

The PHA must undertake the following forms of resident engagement during the conversion process:[1]

1. Prior to submitting a RAD application, the PHA must provide written notification in the form of a RAD Information Notice (RIN) to residents (and applicable resident organizations[2]) of the affected project(s) of the PHA's conversion plans and of the residents' rights in connection with the conversion.[3] Such notification is required even if relocation is not anticipated. The PHA must also provide any required notices when required by the Uniform Relocation Act (URA).[4] "Additionally, HUD encourages PHAs to partner with resident leaders to help communicate information about the RAD conversion to the broader resident population through peer-to-peer engagement[.]"[5]

2. No less than one (1) week following issuance of the RIN and within least six (6) months prior to submission of the RAD application, the PHA must hold at least two (2) meetings

---

1 *See* Section II of Notice H-2023-08 PIH 2023-19 (HA) (Issued July 27, 2023) (Supplemental Notice 4B), which modifies REV-4 Notice.
2 Notice to the resident organization(s) must comply with 24 C.F.R. Part 964. *Id.*
3 *Id.*
4 *See id.*
5 *Id.*

with the residents of the proposed RAD project(s) to discuss the conversion plans and offer residents the opportunity to comment.[6] These meetings must cover, at a minimum:

a. description of the residents' rights;

b. primary differences for residents between public housing and the Section 8 platform (PBV or PBRA) selected for the conversion;

c. the PHA's preliminary intentions, to the extent formulated, with respect to:

   i. whether the proposed project will include transfers of assistance to a different site(s) and the potential site(s) to which assistance would be transferred;

   ii. plans to partner with an entity other than the PHA;

   iii. any change in the number or configuration of assisted units or any other change that could impact a resident's ability to reoccupy to the project following repairs or construction;

   iv. de minimis reduction of units that will have been vacant for more than twenty-four (24) months at the time of RAD application;

   v. the scope of work and potential relocation scenarios; and

   vi. overview and projected timeline of the conversion process.[7]

3. The PHA's RAD application must include the following documentation related to its initial resident engagement efforts:

a. Certification that the RIN and notice of the tenant meetings have been provided to all residents in accordance with the RAD Notice;

b. summary of meeting attendees and participation by residents, PHA staff, and other attendees;

c. description of the PHA's efforts to promote tenant participation in meetings;

d. meeting agenda(s) and copies of handouts or presentation materials;

e. summary of questions and comments asked in the meetings or submitted by residents and the PHA responses;

---

6 *Id.*
7 *Id.*

 f. identification of how residents who were unable to attend meetings could access materials or submit questions or comments and receive responses;

 g. identification of materials that were shared with residents to communicate resident protections; and

 h. where there is a duly elected resident organization, contact information for at least one elected leader of such organization.[8]

4. Following HUD's approval of the RAD application, as evidenced by CHAP issuance, but before requesting a Concept Call, the PHA must have at least two (2) meetings with the residents to discuss updated conversion plans, the topics covered in the pre-application meetings, and provide information and solicit feedback on planned improvements to the physical structure(s), management, and supportive services, as applicable.[9]

"Meetings should be spaced to provide meaningful updates to residents on the progress of the conversion, to offer opportunities for residents to provide input, and to permit residents to raise questions and concerns. PHAs are encouraged to meet with residents each calendar quarter and to provide access to written materials describing the conversion prior to each meeting."[10]

5. The PHA's Financing Plan must include a summary of questions and comments asked in the meeting or submitted by residents and the PHA responses.[11]

6. HUD may require additional resident meetings after the Concept Call if HUD determines that meetings are warranted.[12] For example, HUD may require additional meetings to provide residents with up-to-date information regarding the conversion.

7. Following RCC issuance, but prior to closing, the PHA must (1) provide residents with written notice that the conversion has been

---

8 *Id.*
9 *Id.*
10 *Id.*
11 *Id.*
12 *Id.*

approved, and (2) hold an additional resident meeting after the notice is issued.[13] In the meeting and in the written notice, the PHA must detail the anticipated timing of the conversion; the anticipated duration of the construction or rehabilitation work, if any; the revised terms of the lease and house rules; procedures for execution of the new lease; any anticipated relocation; and opportunities and procedures for the exercise of the Choice-Mobility option.[14] The PHA must also provide residents with access to or copies of the new form of lease and any applicable house rules.[15] The PHA must provide HUD with evidence of the notice and required meeting(s) prior to closing.[16]

8. From RCC issuance and continuing through completion of the RAD scope of work, the PHA must also satisfy a number of statutory, regulatory, and programmatic requirements governing relocation procedures and the preservation of resident rights, depending on the specifics of the particular RAD transaction.[17]

9. Any substantial change to the conversion plans presented in previous resident meetings also triggers a need for additional resident consultation meetings within three (3) months following the change.[18]

---

13 *Id.*
14 *Id.*
15 *Id.*
16 *Id.*
17 *Id.*
18 *Id.*

Application Submission

4

HUD accepts applications on a rolling basis and will continue to award CHAPs as long as units remain available under the RAD Unit Cap or until the Program Sunset Date, whichever occurs first.[1] If additional units become available for conversion under the RAD Unit Cap—when existing RAD awards are declined by PHAs or rescinded by HUD for failure to meet key milestones—then HUD may award additional CHAPs.[2] CHAPs for units up to the RAD Unit Cap will be issued for those applications meeting all HUD's threshold eligibility requirements.[3] HUD will rank each eligible application by the date and time of submission.[4] If HUD has reached the RAD Unit Cap, then the next ranked application will be placed on the RAD waiting list by date and time of submission.[5]

The PHA may apply to convert a set of projects over time or over several phases,[6] locking in the contract rent that is applicable for the year the RAD application is filed. To do so, the PHA must provide HUD with (1) the total number of units to be converted,

---

1 *See* Pub. L. No. 115–141. The congressionally authorized cap was not reached as of the date of publication of this Guide.

2 REV-4 Notice, at 100.

3 *Id*. at 99.

4 *Id*.

5 *Id*.

6 *Id*. at 96–98. (The RAD Notice no longer distinguishes between multi-phase development awards and portfolio awards. PHAs seeking to apply for multi-phase development awards may now do so under the portfolio application.)

and (2) RAD applications for the lesser of four (4) projects or twenty-five percent (25%) of the units identified in the portfolio.[7]

In addition to the issuance of a CHAP, HUD will issue a Portfolio Award Letter, identifying the remaining units in the portfolio that are not covered by the CHAP and confirming the contract rent applicable to those same units. RAD applications for the remaining units must be submitted to HUD by the Program Sunset Date.[8]

The key elements of a RAD application are:

1. **HUD Form of Application (with attachments and narratives).** The RAD application is a web-based form available on the RAD Resource Desk. When the PHA first selects the relevant project in the application form, several application fields will already be pre-populated by the HUD data systems.

   HUD has streamlined the current form of application as much as possible, only requiring the PHA to fill in summary information regarding the tentative plans for the project(s). The application also includes a number of attachments, as described later, with most including language stating that the signatory of the document is aware of and will comply with all relevant RAD policies.

2. **PHA Board Approval.** The RAD application requires certification of approval by the PHA's board. The certification must be executed by an authorized representative of the PHA.[9]

3. **Summary of Resident Comments and PHA Responses.** The PHA must submit a summary of its comprehensive written responses prepared in response to comments received in connection with each of the required resident meetings on the proposed conversions, as further described in Chapter Three.

4. **Mixed-Finance Affidavit.** If the project slated for RAD conversion is a mixed-finance property owned by an entity other than the PHA, the PHA and the current property owner must execute an affidavit

---

7 *Id.* at 97.
8 *Id.* at 96–98.
9 *Id.* at 121.

confirming that if the project is approved for RAD, the project's subsidy will convert to long-term Section 8 rental assistance, comply with the RAD Notice and related requirements, and they will execute the agreements necessary to carry out the RAD conversion, including a HAP contract.

5. **Choice-Mobility Commitment Letter.** For projects converting to PBRA, the Choice-Mobility commitment letter must also be submitted, which confirms that the converted project will provide the Choice-Mobility option described in Section 1.7.C.5 of the RAD Notice. This type of Choice-Mobility option is not a feature of the general PBRA approach and requires that PBRA residents wishing to move from the converted site be provided a TBV upon the later of (1) twenty-four (24) months after the HAP effective date or (2) twenty-four (24) months after the resident moved into the unit.[10] No more than one-third (1/3) of the voucher agency's turnover vouchers may be provided to RAD residents.[11] While not required, a project owner and voucher agency may also implement a per-project cap for vouchers of no more than fifteen percent (15%) of the units within a particular project.[12] Under limited circumstances, HUD also has the authority to grant good-cause exemptions from the Choice-Mobility requirement for up to ten percent (10%) of the overall units converted under RAD.[13]

6. **Transaction Financing and Structure Features.** Depending on the Financing Plan for the conversion, the RAD application may also include the following.[14]

   a. *Bundled Rents.* A PHA may propose to combine the subsidies associated with multiple sites slated for RAD conversion in order to set rents at varying levels across these sites in a manner that does not exceed the aggregate amount of subsidy available upon conversion.

---

10 *Id.* at 89.

11 *Id.*

12 *Id.* at 89–90.

13 *Id.* at 90–91.

14 *Id.* at 96–99; see also id. at 38–41 describing financing considerations, which include the use of Low-Income Housing Tax Credits, Housing Tax Credits, Opportunity Zones, and other state or local tax incentive structures to support recapitalization.

To do so, the application must include a calculation that shows that the total subsidy applied to the various projects does not exceed the aggregate funding level.[15]

b. *Moving to Work (MTW) Contract Rent Flexibility*.[16] When submitting RAD applications for two or more projects, PHAs designated as MTW agencies may utilize their ability to combine subsidy streams under block grant authority when setting initial contract rents (thus augmenting rents beyond the contract rents otherwise available under RAD). To do so, the PHA must use existing MTW funds to supplement the initial contract rents and identify the additional subsidy in its RAD application, and the investment of MTW block grant funds will require HUD perform a subsidy layering review.[17] MTW agencies will also remain subject to the requirement that they serve substantially the same number of families as would have been served if the PHA was not an MTW agency.[18]

As a general matter, conversions by MTW PHAs using a PBRA HAP contract will be administered outside the PHA's MTW authority, while PBV conversions will be incorporated into the PHA's MTW program in a manner consistent with the RAD Notice.[19]

c. *Portfolio Applications*. A PHA may apply to convert a single project over multiple phases or multiple projects over time, locking in the contract rent that is applicable for the year each RAD application is filed. To do so, the PHA must provide HUD with (1) a list of all projects proposed for inclusion in the portfolio award (including the project name, PIC development number, units to be converted, total estimated capital needs, and major anticipated

---

15 *Id.* at 54–55.

16 REV-4 Notice at § 1.6.B.5.f (for PBV) and § 1.7.B.5.f (for PBRA) provides opportunities to non-MTW PHAs to augment the initial rent for Repair–Restore units (referred to as Faircloth-to-RAD in the REV-4 Notice). The opportunity to augment PBV Repair–Restore initial rents ended on September 30, 2024, while the opportunity to augment PBRA Repair–Restore initial rents is ongoing. Future guidance may permit augmentation for initial rents for PBV Repair–Restore initial rents.

17 REV-4 Notice, at 54.

18 *Id.*; *see also* Notice PIH 2013-02 (HA).

19 Notice PIH 2012-32 (HA), REV-1, § 1.5.F.

funding sources; and (2) RAD applications for at least 25% of the units identified in the portfolio award. Together with the issuance of a CHAP, HUD will provide the PHA a Portfolio Award Letter identifying the remaining units in the portfolio that are not covered by the CHAP and confirming the contract rent applicable to those same units.[20]

d. *Justification for More than a De Minimis Reduction in Units.* If the PHA proposes to reduce the number of assisted units that will remain in place following conversion beyond the de minimis amount as allowed by the Notice (defined as the greater of five percent (5%) and five (5) units), the PHA must describe the proposed reduction and identify which of the three special exceptions allowed by the Notice the PHA is relying upon for the reduction.[21]

---

20 *Id.* at 97–99; *see* Attachment IC.

21 *Id.* at 26–27 (describing the three exceptions permitting more than a de minimis reduction as (a) the unit previously received a Section 18 demolition or disposition approval; (b) the unit has been vacant for more than 24 months; and (c) reducing the number of units will allow the PHA to "more effectively or efficiently serve assisted households through: 1) reconfiguring apartments . . . 2) facilitating social service delivery . . .").

Statutory and Regulatory Waivers and Considerations | 5

As permitted by statute, the RAD Notice waives a number of regulations and statutory requirements, while stressing the continued applicability of others or imposing alternative requirements. The key waivers and significant requirements that continue in effect or are newly applied within the RAD context are described next.

Statutory and Regulatory Waivers

1. **Use of Public Housing Funds to Support Conversion.** Typically, public housing Operating Funds and Capital Funds may only support public housing units or pay for public housing-related costs. However, HUD has made public housing funds available to support units undergoing RAD conversion, but those funds must be identified in the Financing Plan and the RCC.

   Public housing funds can be used to pay the following costs associated with a RAD conversion: predevelopment costs; development costs; establishment of replacement and/or operating reserves; and payment of Capital Fund Financing Program, Operating Fund Financing Program, or Energy Performance Contract debt.[1]

---

1 REV-4 Notice, at 43. (A PHA may spend up to $100,000 in public housing funds for pre-development costs without HUD approval.)

HUD will extend the obligation deadline for public housing Capital Funds for up to three (3) years from the previous obligation end date.[2] As a result the expenditure end dates benefit from corresponding extensions.[3]

PHAs have discretion in setting the amount of public housing funds allocated to a RAD project upon conversion. Allocations that exceed the average amount of funds the converted project held in its operating reserves over the prior three (3) years and any contribution of Capital Funds, inclusive of Replacement Housing Factor (RHF) funds, will trigger a subsidy-layering review consistent with 24 C.F.R. § 4.13.[4]

The RAD Notice also requires PHAs to use public housing Operating Funds and Capital Funds to make HAP payments for the initial calendar year of the HAP contract.

2. **Public Housing Disposition and/or Demolition.** It is not necessary to obtain disposition or demolition approval under Section 18 of the Housing Act (Section 18) if the number of units assisted under RAD is no more than a de minimis reduction from the number of public housing units in place before the RAD conversion. For this purpose, HUD defines "de minimis" as the greater of five percent (5%) of the number of public housing units that existed immediately prior to the conversion or five (5) units.[5]

The RAD Notice also allows a reduction beyond the de minimis amount for (1) any units that have been vacant for twenty-four (24) months or longer at the time of the RAD application; or (2) those units whose reduction will allow the PHA to serve residents more effectively or efficiently through unit reconfiguration or the facilitation of social service delivery.[6]

---

2 *Id.*

3 *Id.*

4 *Id.* at 44.

5 *Id.* at 26. For example, the need for Section 18 disposition approval does not apply to a project involving 100 public housing units, provided at least 95 units are assisted after the conversion.

6 *Id.* (Note that the REV-4 Notice expanded the definition of "de minimis" to encompass those units that were considered exceptions to the Section 18 disposition or demolition approval requirement in the initial notice.)

Otherwise, the PHA must obtain approval under Section 18 to reduce its number of assisted units.

3. **Joint RAD and Section 18 Applications.** HUD will allow the PHA to combine RAD and Section 18 in a single project under certain circumstances where (1) the hard construction costs for the planned rehabilitation or new construction at the project exceed HUD-determined thresholds, and the project does not use nine percent (9%) low-income housing tax credits;[7] (b) the PHA seeks to pursue RAD and Section 18 approval simultaneously to dispose of its last fifty (50) or fewer public housing units;[8] or (3) the PHA seeks to use Section 18 approval to dispose of other units at the Converting Project to allow more efficient or effective on-site or off-site development.[9] Under all circumstances, the PHA should submit a RAD application for all units at the project. If HUD determines that the PHA is eligible to combine RAD and Section 18, HUD will offer a streamlined process to approve the Section 18 eligible units.[10] See Chapter 12 for further detail about the RAD/Section 18 Blend.

4. **Asset Repositioning Fees and RHF Funds.** A disposition of public housing units would typically generate asset repositioning fees under 24 C.F.R. § 990.190(h) and provide access to RHF funds or Demolition and Disposition Transitional Funding (DDTF) funds pursuant to 24 C.F.R. § 905.400(i) and (j), respectively. However, such resources are not generated as a result of the disposition of public housing units through RAD unless the conversion is a RAD/Section 18 Blend.[11] Nonetheless, the PHA may access existing asset repositioning fees and RHF/DDTF funding to financially support conversion of units under RAD.

---

7 *See* PIH Notice 2021-07 (issued Jan. 19, 2021) and Section VII of Supplemental Notice 4B.

8 *See* PIH Notice 2021-07 and REV-4 at 45.

9 REV-4 at 45.

10 *Id.*

11 *See* PIH Notice 2021-07 and REV-4 at 45, as modified by Notice H-2025-01 PIH 2025-03 (HA) (issued Jan. 16, 2025) (Supplemental Notice 4C), which modifies REV-4 Notice and Supplemental Notice 4B.

5. **Reduction in Faircloth Limit.** PHAs are permitted to construct and/or support new public housing units up to a certain amount as prescribed by Section 9(g)(3) of the Housing Act to the number of public housing units owned, assisted, or operated by the PHA as of October 1, 1999 (Faircloth Limit). Typically, demolition or disposition of public housing units creates room under the Faircloth Limit, enabling the PHA to later construct and/or support new public housing units. Notwithstanding Section 9(g)(3), conversion under RAD results in a permanent reduction in the number of public housing units authorized under the Faircloth Limit.[12]

6. **Resident Opportunities and Self-Sufficiency Service Coordinators (ROSS) and Public Housing Family Self-Sufficiency (FSS) Programs.** The RAD Notice waives provisions in Section 23 and Section 34 of the Housing Act to enable public housing residents to continue to participate in ROSS and FSS programs,[13] as further discussed in Chapter 6.

7. **Public Housing Assessment System (PHAS).** The RAD Notice exempts projects for which a CHAP has been issued and an Inventory Management System/Public and Indian Housing Information Center (PIC) removal application has been accepted from the PHAS scoring process for the fiscal year in which the PIC Removal Application (as such term is defined in Chapter 8) is accepted and for every fiscal year thereafter.[14]

8. **Section 33 Conversion Review.** The RAD Notice waives the requirement that the PHA undertake an annual review under the Section 33 required conversion process for projects that have been issued a CHAP or are covered by a portfolio award.[15]

---

12 *Id.* at 46–47. Prior notices excluded de minimis units from the Faircloth Limit reduction. The current notice applies this provision to all public housing units, retroactive to all RAD conversions.

13 *Id.* at 48.

14 *Id.* at 49.

15 *Id.* at 51.

Additional Statutory and Regulatory Considerations

1. **Significant Amendment.** Actions implemented under RAD require that the PHA's board approve a significant amendment to the PHA's Five-Year Plan, Annual Plan, and MTW Plan for MTW agencies with standard MTW agreements.[16] HUD prescribes the contents of the significant amendment at Attachment 1D of the RAD Notice. The PHA's Five-Year Plan, Annual Plan, MTW Plan, or Significant Amendment thereto, as applicable, must be submitted with the Financing Plan.[17]

2. **Green Building, Energy-Efficiency Standards, and Climate Resilience.** The RAD Notice promotes green building and energy-efficiency standards. For example, any retrofit projects involving the replacement of systems and appliances must be done with, at minimum, products certified under Energy Star, WaterSense, or the Federal Energy Management Program, or the most energy- and water-efficient options that are financially feasible and identified as cost effective by the CNA. The CNA will analyze energy-saving options and green building elements, which will then be used, in turn, to assist with identifying the scope of rehabilitation.[18] New construction must meet or exceed either the 2021 International Energy Conservation Code or the ASHRAE 90.1-2019 standard or successor code deemed feasible by HUD under the Energy Independence Act of 2007. The RAD Notice also encourages new construction projects to meet or exceed the requirements for Energy Star for New Homes or Energy Star for Multifamily New Construction.[19] Supplemental Notice 4B and Supplemental Notice 4C also set forth HUD's latest requirements related to analysis of the project's climate hazard risks and disaster planning in the event such risks materialize.

---

16 *Id.* at 47. (A significant amendment is only required if the RAD conversion plans are not fully discussed in the PHA's Five-Year Plan, Annual Plan, or MTW Plan.)

17 *Id.*

18 *Id.* at 25.

19 *Id.*

3. **Relocation.** Should relocation be required as part of the RAD conversion, it must be undertaken in accordance with the URA and the applicable regulations at 49 C.F.R. Part 24, and any additional requirements that may be applicable, such as Section 104(d) of the Housing and Community Development Act of 1974.[20] Relocation is discussed further in Chapter 7.

4. **Accessibility Requirements.** The RAD Notice provides that Section 504 of the Rehabilitation Act of 1973, the Americans with Disabilities Act, and the Fair Housing Act apply to all conversions, whether they involve new construction, alterations, or existing facilities.[21]

5. **Site Selection and Neighborhood Standards.** Any construction of units on an alternate site using RAD-related assistance will require compliance with the site selection requirements of the Fair Housing Act and Title VI of the Civil Rights Act of 1964.[22]

6. **HUD Access to Records.** PHAs are required to agree to "any reasonable HUD request for data to support program evaluation." This could include project financial statements, operating data, Choice-Mobility utilization, and rehabilitation work.[23] The need to provide access to these records is tied to language in the RAD statute requiring that HUD "demonstrate the feasibility of this conversion model to recapitalize and operate public housing properties" and "assess and publish findings regarding the impact of the conversion of assistance under the demonstration on the preservation and improvement of public housing, the amount of private sector leveraging as a result of such conversion, and the effect of such conversion on tenants."[24] PBRA projects are also required to provide HUD year-end financial statements as required by 24 C.F.R. Part 5, subpart H.[25]

---

20 *Id.* at 27.

21 *Id.* at 28–29.

22 *Id.* at 29 (also applying implementing regulations at 24 C.F.R. §§ 1.4(b)(3) and 983.57 for PBV projects or Appendix III of REV-4 Notice for PBRA projects).

23 *Id.* at 69, 87.

24 2012 Appropriations Act.

25 REV-4 Notice, at 91.

7. **Additional Monitoring Requirements.** The RAD Notice requires that the PHA board approve the operating budget for PBV projects on an annual basis, confirm that the project owner is making deposits into the replacement reserve account in accordance with the RCC, and assess the financial health of the project.[26]

8. **Davis-Bacon and Section 3 Requirements.** Notwithstanding the fact that the Davis-Bacon rules[27] and Section 3 resident employment and economic opportunity requirements[28] do not apply to existing housing under 24 C.F.R. § 983.52(a), the RAD Notice imposes these requirements on all work identified in the project's Financing Plan and RCC that qualifies as "development."[29] Development includes work that begins within eighteen (18) months of the HAP contract's effective date and constitutes remodeling that alters the nature or type of housing units, reconstruction, or a substantial improvement in the quality or kind of original equipment or materials.[30]

9. **Waiting Lists.** The RAD Notice provides guidance for (1) the PHA in establishing and maintaining a voucher-wide, program-wide, or site-based waiting list for PBV conversions[31] and (2) the project owner in utilizing a project-specific or community waiting list for PBRA conversions.[32] The PHA shall have discretion in deciding the best means to transition applicants from the current public housing waiting list.[33] If the assistance is being transferred to another site as part of the RAD conversion and the existing project uses a project-specific waiting list, then the PHA shall notify those on the waiting list of the transfer, inform them about how they can apply for residency at the new site,

---

26 *Id.* at 69.

27 *See* Section 12 of the U.S. Housing Act of 1937.

28 *See* Section 3 of the Housing and Urban Development Act of 1968, as implemented at 24 C.F.R. Part 135.

29 REV-4 Notice, at 37. Davis-Bacon requirements will only be applied to projects with nine or more units.

30 *Id.*

31 *Id.* at 69. 24 C.F.R. § 983.251 sets out the PBV program requirements for establishing the waiting list.

32 *Id.* at 87.

33 *Id.* at 70, 88.

and provide them with a priority ranking on the new project-specific waiting list based on the date and time of their application to the existing project's list.[34]

For projects where a project-specific waiting list does not exist, the PHA must establish a waiting list in accordance with 24 C.F.R. § 903.7(b)(2)(ii)–(iv). The RAD Notice lends discretion to PHAs in determining how to inform applicants on the public housing waiting list when establishing the waiting list for a particular RAD project.[35] The RAD Notice offers considerations for PHAs to take into account when reaching out to residents on the public housing waiting list.

10. **Mandatory Insurance Coverage.** The RAD Notice does not prescribe specific levels of insurance but indicates that the converted project must always maintain "commercially available property and liability insurance," and that, to the extent there are sufficient insurance proceeds, it must "promptly restore, reconstruct, and/or repair any damaged or destroyed property of a project."[36] This language conflicts with the level of control senior lenders and/or tax credit investors seek to exercise regarding the application of insurance proceeds and decisions about restoration, and it is unclear at this point the extent to which HUD will defer to senior lender requirements. The conflict can be addressed through language added to the lender and investor documents acknowledging that the HUD requirements control.

11. **Future Refinancing.** Any refinancing or restructuring of permanent debt during the term of the HAP contract requires HUD approval. HUD will seek to ensure that the financing supports long-term preservation of the converted housing.[37]

---

34 *Id.* The RAD Notice provides such requirements where, due to the site transfer, the applicant would only be eligible for a unit in a location that is materially different from the location they applied to.

35 *Id.*

36 *Id.* at 71, 89.

37 *Id.* at 71, 91.

Resident Protections

6

The RAD Notice provides certain resident protections applicable to both PBV and PBRA projects, with a few slight variations between the two types.[1] HUD's joint notice H2014-09/PHA 2014-17 issued on July 14, 2014 (Relocation Notice) also provides guidance concerning the resident relocation process and rights under RAD and URA. The essential rights afforded residents are described herein.

No Rescreening of Residents upon Conversion

Given the protections in the RAD statute, existing residents are not subject to rescreening, income eligibility, or income targeting.[2] Thus, an existing, over-income household is allowed to remain in the unit after the conversion. The unit, when the over-income household vacates, must then be leased to an income eligible household. To implement this requirement, HUD is waiving 24 C.F.R. § 982.201 and Section 8(o)(4) of the Housing Act in the

---

1 REV-4 Notice § 1.6.C (relating to PBV projects), § 1.7.B (relating to PBRA projects).

2 2012 Appropriations Act (providing in part, "notwithstanding sections 3 and 16 of the [U.S. Housing Act of 1937], the conversion of assistance under the demonstration shall not be the basis for re-screening or termination of assistance or eviction of any tenant family in a property participating in the demonstration, and such a family shall not be considered a new admission for any purpose, including compliance with income-targeting requirements").

PBV context and the first clause of Section 8(c)(4) of the Housing Act and 24 C.F.R. § 880.603(b) in the PBRA context.[3] If the Financing Plan for the RAD conversion involves low-income housing tax credits, the RAD requirement that prevents rescreening for income eligibility poses a conflict with Section 42 of the Internal Revenue Code since the RAD statutory language does not sufficiently waive the need for all tax-credit units to be occupied when such units are placed in service by households with incomes at or below sixty percent (60%) of the area median income.[4] The PHA may choose to exclude such over-income units from the applicable financing programs.[5]

Resident Participation

Residents of Covered Projects maintain the right to establish and operate resident organizations in accordance with 24 C.F.R. Part 245. Project owners are required to collect funds annually at $25 for each occupied unit to be distributed to resident organizations that provide resident education and organize around tenancy issues.[6] Where no resident organization is established, the project owner and residents are encouraged to work together in fostering a working relationship, which may include guidance on how to form a resident organization.[7] Regardless, funds must be collected by the project owner and made available for residents upon written request of such funds.[8]

Resident organizations have certain protected rights under the RAD Notice, including leafletting/flyering around communal spaces, door-to-door

---

3 REV-4 Notice, at 60–61, 80.

4 26 U.S.C. § 42(g)(1)(D)(i) (stating, "notwithstanding an increase in the income of the occupants of a low-income unit above the income limitation applicable under paragraph (1), such units shall continue to be treated as a low-income unit of the income of such occupants initially met such income limitation and such unit continues to be rent-restricted"). The ability to maintain an over-income resident in a low-income housing tax credit unit and to continue to consider such a unit to be low-income housing tax-credit-eligible is dependent on the resident having initially met the income limits. If a resident in the RAD project earns over the income limit at the point the unit is placed in service for purposes of Section 42 of the Internal Revenue Code, it is unlikely the unit will qualify as a low-income unit necessary to generate the tax credit.

5 Relocation Notice § 6.2.

6 REV-4 Notice, Attachment 1B.

7 *Id.*

8 *Id.*

surveying, holding regularly scheduled meetings in space that is provided by the project owner, formulating responses on project owner's requests to increase rent, major capital additions, and other such concerns that impact the building.[9]

Public housing residents who are participants of the FSS or ROSS programs may continue their participation in the Covered Projects for the duration of the grant's period of performance.[10] Project owners must notify HUD when there are FSS participants in the Covered Project, and are required to administer the FSS program directly or partner with another agency to administer the program in accordance with 24 C.F.R. Part 984. Further, when a Covered Project has FSS participants, the project owner is required to take on the administrative duties associated with the program, including calculating and crediting escrow and reporting.[11] Such reporting requirements may differ under the HCV program or a public housing resident.[12] Project owners are not required to recruit new participants in the FSS program.

ROSS participants may use the remainder of the ROSS grant money once the project is converted under RAD. PHAs or project owners, including those who were ineligible for grant renewal prior to the effective date of Supplemental Notice 4C, may apply for additional ROSS grant funding for a Covered Project, subject to the requirements of the applicable ROSS Notice of Funding Opportunity.[13]

Resident Right to Return

Should the RAD conversion involve rehabilitation or construction work requiring temporary relocation of the residents, such residents will be afforded the right to return to the converted project once rehabilitation or construction is complete. Should the assistance be transferred to a new

---

9 *Id.*

10 REV-4 Notice, at 62, 82.

11 *Id.*

12 *Id.*

13 *Id.*

site,[14] the residents of the converted project will be entitled to occupy an assisted unit at that new site. If a resident desires to permanently relocate to another assisted unit outside of the RAD conversion, the resident may waive his or her right to occupy the converted unit following completion of rehabilitation or construction.[15]

The Relocation Notice allows the PHA to present proposed plans that could preclude a resident from returning to the converted project, but must permit the resident a chance to review and comment upon or object to the proposal. Should the resident object to the proposal, the PHA must adjust the plan to permit the resident to continue to live at the site following the RAD conversion.[16] If the plans precluding a resident's return are acceptable to the resident impacted by such plans, the resident must provide the PHA with informed, written consent to receive voluntary permanent relocation assistance and other payments as required by the URA, acknowledging that acceptance of such assistance terminates the resident's right to return to the converted project and must be signed by the head of the household.[17] The Relocation Notice stresses the need to provide residents with 30-day notice informing them of the right to return and relocation possibilities, as well as temporary and permanent housing options. Such notice must be provided in a way that does not pressure a resident to forgo their right to return or to accept relocation assistance.[18] PHAs also must maintain records of information provided to residents and any related consents from residents. HUD indicates it is possible HUD will request such records when reviewing the PHA's Fair Housing and Equal Opportunity (FHEO) Relocation and Accessibility Checklist or when addressing any future relocation issues.[19]

---

14 REV-4 Notice, at 60, 80. The Notice also requires that HUD find that the transfer of assistance to a new site is warranted and provide approval of such transfer.

15 *Id.*

16 Relocation Notice § 6.2.

17 *Id.*; voluntary permanent relocation must abide by the provisions in Section 6.10 of the Relocation Notice.

18 *Id.*

19 *Id.*

Relocation 7

When the need for temporary or permanent relocation of residents arises, the PHA and/or project owner should plan for such relocation as to reasonably minimize any disruption to residents' lives; ensure that residents are not exposed to unsafe living conditions; and comply with applicable relocation, fair housing, and civil rights requirements.[1] In Chapter 6 we reviewed the resident's rights to return. This chapter will focus on the notice requirements and the relocation planning by the PHA and/or project owner.

Relocation Assistance and Resident Notice

RAD requires that the affected residents receive either permanent or temporary relocation assistance as determined by the duration of relocation.[2] Both permanent and temporary relocation assistance cover reimbursement of all reasonable out-of-pocket expenses incurred in connection with the relocation.[3]

---

1 Relocation Notice § 6.

2 *Id.* § 6.4. Note that the definition of "permanent" varies between the RAD Notice and Relocation Notice. For example the Relocation Notice considers any transfer lasting over a year to be a permanent relocation; however, the RAD Notice finds a permanent relocation when the resident is separated from the RAD-assisted unit after conversion. Thus, if a resident is moving to retain a RAD-assisted unit, there is no permanent relocation.

3 *Id.* § 6.4A. The Relocation Notice explains that temporary relocation assistance includes but is not limited to moving expenses, any increase in housing costs

The PHA must provide residents at least thirty (30) days to elect either permanent or temporary relocation assistance. By electing permanent relocation assistance under the URA, a resident is forgoing the right to return to the RAD project following conversion and/or completion of any construction work.[4] For purposes of URA assistance, a resident becomes eligible for such assistance upon the initiation of negotiations (ION). The Relocation Notice sets the issuance date of the RCC as the ION date.[5] Given the timing for issuance of the RCC and the need to provide residents at least thirty (30) days to elect either permanent or temporary relocation, an initial determination about which relocation option will likely need to occur well before the ION date.

Should a temporary relocation extend beyond a year, the PHA must offer the affected resident permanent relocation assistance under the URA.[6] Should the resident elect such assistance, the resident will also not be eligible to return to the RAD project. The resident may, however, choose to remain temporarily relocated and ultimately return to the RAD project upon completion.[7]

Resident Notification

In addition to the required outreach to residents before submitting its RAD application, the PHA and/or the entity undertaking the RAD conversion in collaboration with the PHA must provide a series of notices to residents. They are fully described in the Relocation Notice and summarized as follows.

1. **RAD Information Notice**
   As noted in Chapter 3, the RIN must be issued before the RAD application is submitted. The RIN should be incorporated into the initial

---

during the relocation period, meals if the temporary housing lacks cooking facilities, and other applicable expenses. *Id.* § 6.4B.

4 *Id.* The right to return is described in more detail in Chapter 6.

5 *Id.* § 6.5.

6 *Id.* § 6.4(C). Any URA assistance would be provided in addition to temporary relocation assistance and would not be offset by the amount of previously provided temporary relocation assistance. *Id.*

7 Relocation Notice § 6.4. As long as the resident does not accept permanent relocation assistance under the URA, the resident preserves the right to return to the RAD project.

resident consultation process and, as described in the Relocation Notice, it must at minimum provide the following:

- Provide a general description of the conversion transaction (e.g., the Converting Project, whether the PHA anticipates any new construction or transfer of assistance, whether the PHA anticipates partnering with a developer or other entity to implement the transaction);
- Inform the resident that early conceptual plans are likely to change as the PHA gathers more information, including, among other items, resident opinions, and an analysis of the capital needs of the property and financing options;
- Inform the resident that the household has a right to remain in the unit or, if any relocation is required, a right to return to an assisted unit in the Covered Project (which may be at the new site in the case of a transfer of assistance);
- Inform the resident that they will not be subject to any rescreening as a result of the conversion;[8]
- Inform the resident that the household cannot be required to move permanently without the resident's consent, except in the case of a transfer of assistance when the resident may be required to move a reasonable distance, as determined by HUD, in order to follow the assisted unit;
- Inform the resident that if any relocation is involved in the transaction, the resident is entitled to relocation protections under the requirements of the RAD program and, in some circumstances, the requirements of the URA, which protections may include advance written notice of any move, advisory services, payment(s), and other assistance as applicable to the situation;

---

8 As noted earlier in this chapter, if the Financing Plan for the RAD conversion involves low-income housing tax credits, the RAD requirement that prevents rescreening for income eligibility poses a conflict with Section 42 of the Internal Revenue Code since the RAD statutory language does not sufficiently waive the need for all tax-credit units to be occupied when such units are placed in service by households with incomes at or below sixty percent (60%) of the area median income. The PHA may choose to exclude such over-income units from the applicable financing programs. Relocation Notice § 6.2.

- Inform the resident that any resident-initiated move from the Converting Project could put any future relocation payment(s) and assistance at risk and instruct the resident not to move from the Converting Project; and
- Inform the resident that the RAD transaction will be completed consistent with fair housing and civil rights requirements, and provide contact information to process reasonable accommodation requests for residents with disabilities during relocation.[9]

2. **General Information Notice**

Where a General Information Notice (GIN) is required,[10] the Relocation Notice mandates that it must be provided as soon feasible. For any RAD conversions involving acquisition, rehabilitation, or demolition, this shall be no later than thirty (30) days after CHAP issuance.[11] For RAD conversions, the GIN must at least:

- Inform the resident that he or she may be displaced from the project and generally describe the relocation payment(s) for which the resident may be eligible, the basic conditions of eligibility, and the procedures for obtaining the payment(s);
- Inform the resident that, if he or she qualifies for relocation assistance as a displaced person under the URA, he or she will be given reasonable relocation advisory services, including referrals to replacement properties, help in filing payment claims, and other necessary assistance to help the displaced resident successfully relocate;
- Inform the resident that, if they qualify for relocation assistance as a displaced person under the URA, they:
  - will not be required to move without ninety (90) days' advance written notice, and
  - cannot be required to move permanently unless at least one comparable replacement dwelling has been made available;

---

9 *Id.* § 6.6A.

10 *Id.* § 6.6B. A GIN will be provided to individuals who may be displaced due to federally assisted projects involving acquisition, rehabilitation, or demolition.

11 *Id.* Provided that acquisition, rehabilitation, or demolition was anticipated at the time of the CHAP. Otherwise, as soon as feasible following the change in project plans.

- Inform the resident that any person who is an alien not lawfully present in the United States is ineligible for relocation advisory services and relocation payments, unless such ineligibility would result in exceptional and extremely unusual hardship to a qualifying spouse, parent, or child (see 49 C.F.R. § 24.208(h) for additional information);
- Describe the resident's right to appeal the PHA's determination as to a resident's eligibility for URA assistance; and
- Inform the resident that the RAD transaction will be completed consistent with fair housing and civil rights requirements and provide contact information to process reasonable accommodation requests for residents with disabilities during the relocation.[12]

3. RAD Notice of Relocation

With receipt of the RCC (i.e., the ION date), the PHA must, in accordance with the Relocation Notice, provide residents with at least thirty (30) days' notice of the pending relocation.[13] Should the RAD conversion not require relocation, the Relocation Notice suggests that the PHA notify residents that they will not be relocated.[14] As outlined in the Relocation Notice, the RAD Notice of Relocation must:

- Identify the expected length of the resident's relocation;
- Provide at least thirty (30) days' advance notice before a temporary relocation, and a possibly longer notice for residents relocated for a longer period of time (e.g., a relocation of six (6) months or more);
- Explain that residents who will be temporarily relocated for more than a year will have at least thirty (30) days to elect either a temporary or permanent relocation as noted earlier;[15]

---

12 *Id.*

13 *Id.* § 6.6(d). While the Relocation Notice also indicates that in instances involving the acquisition of another site as part of the RAD process, a PHA or an acquiring entity may issue the RAD Notice of Relocation together with the Notice of Intent to acquire before the ION date to allow residents who elect permanent relocation sufficient time to receive ninety (90) days advanced written notice of relocation, HUD appears to suggest that it is not permissible to issue the RAD Notice of Relocation before the ION date. *Id.* As a practical matter, when a RAD closing is anticipated to occur within a close timeframe following the RCC issuance, timing constraints may result, and the closing date delayed if the RAD Notice of Relocation cannot be issued before the ION date.

14 *Id.*

15 A PHA can issue the 30-day RAD Notice of Relocation with the 90-day URA notice of permanent relocation at the same time, provided the resident is provided at least one

- Provide at least ninety (90) days' advance notice for any permanent relocation, including any residents who will be relocated for more than a year, which ninety (90) days can begin after the resident has been provided at least one comparable replacement dwelling unit;
- Describe the available relocation assistance, the estimated amount of the assistance, and the procedures for obtaining the assistance in a manner specific to the particular resident's situation to ensure that the resident is clear about what type and amount of assistance to which the household may be entitled;
- Describe the "reasonable terms and conditions" under which the resident may continue to occupy a unit in the completed project; and
- Indicate that the PHA will reimburse the resident for all reasonable out-of-pocket expenses incurred in connection with the temporary relocation (e.g., moving expenses and increased housing costs for rent, utilities).[16]

4. **Notice of Intent to Acquire**

If a project involves the acquisition of an additional site, the Relocation Notice explains that the acquiring entity may issue a Notice of Intent to Acquire (NOIA) before the ION date.[17] The RAD Notice of Relocation would also be issued with the NOIA before the ION date.[18]

5. **URA Notice of Relocation Eligibility**

When a resident's temporary relocation exceeds a year, the PHA must issue the resident a URA-compliant notice of relocation eligibility.[19] This notice must meet the URA requirements set forth at 49 C.F.R. Part 24 and HUD Handbook 1378 as well as the following:

- Provide an updated timeline for the resident's return to the completed project;

---

comparable replacement dwelling unit as required by 49 C.F.R. § 24.204(a). *Id.* § 6.6(d).

16 *Id.*

17 *Id.* § 6.6C (describing that the NOIA may not be issued earlier than ninety (90) days before a reasonable estimated for submission of the PHA's Financing Plan).

18 *Id.*

19 *Id.* § 6.6E. Such notice is not required if the resident previously elected permanent relocation assistance.

- Offer the resident the opportunity to elect to remain temporarily relocated or accept the permanent URA relocation assistance; and
- If the resident chooses permanent relocation assistance and such assistance requires the resident to move, the resident must be provided ninety (90) days' advance written notice of the earliest date upon which they will need to move.[20]

6. **Public Housing Lease Termination Notice**

While not specifically required by or referenced in the RAD Notice, the Relocation Notice alerts PHAs to consider 24 C.F.R. Parts 5 and 966. Application of these regulations within the RAD context presents a number of issues and potential conflicts with the intent and purpose of the resident protections inherent in RAD. For example, the regulations at 24 C.F.R. § 966.4(1)(3)(ii) require that the notice to residents inform them of:

- The termination of their lease;
- The grounds for termination;
- The resident's right to reply to the lease termination notice;
- The resident's right to examine PHA documents directly relevant to the termination or eviction; and
- The resident's right to request a hearing in accordance with the PHA's grievance procedure if the PHA is required to provide the resident with an opportunity for a grievance hearing.

Application of 24 C.F.R. § 966.4(1)(3) addresses a termination of tenancy for a perceived violation of lease terms. Termination within the RAD context is not due to lease violation, but rather to implement the regulatory conversion process. Thus, a grievance process in the traditional sense is not readily applicable, as the RAD conversion process does not involve the termination of a tenancy, but a continuation of a tenancy under a different regulatory scheme and subsidy source. The RAD statute states that "the conversion of assistance under the demonstration shall not be the basis for re-screening

---

20 *Id.* As with any 90-day notice of permanent relocation under the URA, the 90-day window will not commence until the resident has been provided at least one "comparable replacement dwelling" as required by 49 C.F.R. § 24.204(a).

or for a termination of assistance or eviction of any resident family in a property participating in the demonstration."[21] Providing residents with notice of lease termination and then implementing grievance procedures as required by 24 C.F.R. § 966.4(1)(3)(ii) potentially contradicts the public comment process required through RAD that seeks to assure residents of their right to continue their tenancy while overlooking the fact that RAD prohibits terminations of assistance. PHAs and those involved in converting public housing through RAD should consider addressing the notice of public housing lease termination requirements as part of the overall RAD public comment period. The PHA could issue the 30-day notice well in advance of the actual conversion to lend the notice some context and to limit the extent to which residents receive information that could be perceived as contradicting the protections imposed by RAD.

Planning

Where there is a possibility that residents will be relocated from a Converting Project during a RAD transaction, the PHA (or other displacing agency)[22] must undertake a planning process to minimize the adverse impact of the relocation on the residents in accordance with the URA and 49 C.F.R. § 24.205.[23] If the relocation of residents is permanent, including a transfer of assistance, or is a temporary relocation for over a year, the PHA must prepare a written relocation plan.[24] Prior to submitting its Financing Plan, all parts of the PHA's FHEO Relocation and Accessibility Checklist must be submitted to HUD.[25] The PHA is required to meet with residents and solicit feedback throughout the RAD conversion as part of its planning

---

21 2012 Appropriations Act.

22 Under the URA, the term "displacing agency" refers to the entity carrying out a program or project causing a resident to be displaced. The displaying agency may be the project owner or PHA in the Relocation Notice, depending on their role in the transaction. *See* Relocation Notice fn. 66.

23 Relocation Notice § 6.1.

24 *Id.*

25 *Id.*

process.[26] Following is a sample timeline of notifications and requirements a PHA must satisfy in its relocation plan.[27]

Stage	Action(s)
Prior to RAD application submission	Should determine relocation needs and meet with residents to communicate plans, communicate their right to return, and solicit feedback. At this time, RIN should be provided to residents.
After RAD application submission	Prepare the Significant Amendment to PHA Plan, and engage any Resident Advisory Board, residents, and public. Survey residents regarding relocation planning and process.
Issuance of CHAP	Provide GIN to residents if project involves acquisition, rehabilitation, or demolition.
Preparation of Financing Plan	Refine relocation plan and include the construction schedule. PHAs and project owners must seek to minimize any off-site or disruptive relocation activities. At this time, relocation housing options should be identified, and relocation expenses should be budgeted. If required, a relocation plan should be submitted. If required by the project owner, the Notice of Intent to Acquire should be issued.
RCC to Closing	Meet with residents to describe approved conversion plans and to discuss required relocation. The effective date of the RCC begins the ION timeline, as described earlier. Resident relocation may begin as of the effective date of the RCC, subject to notice requirements.
Post-Closing	Notify the residents regarding return to the Covered Project.

If required by the URA, a GIN must also be issued.[28] The URA governs when the GIN must be issued, but if an RIN is required, it must be provided to residents before the PHA submits its RAD application.[29] The Relocation Notice provides that the PHA determine the need for relocation and survey residents to prepare a relocation plan and an estimate of the relocation process cost.[30]

---

26 Relocation Notice § 6.1; *see also* REV-4 Notice § 1.8.
27 *See* Relocation Notice § 6.1.
28 *Id.*
29 REV-4 Notice, at 93.
30 REV-4 Notice § 4; see Chapter 6, *infra*, for a further discussion of relocation requirements and other resident protections.

CHAP Award and Pre-Financing Plan Activities 8

Upon reviewing and approving a RAD application, HUD issues a CHAP.[1] The CHAP identifies the units that will be the subject of the conversion and includes terms on which HUD will later issue the HAP contract.[2]

The CHAP is nonnegotiable, but it may be amended, as needed, to split or combine CHAPs, modify the units or utility allowances, utilize rent flexibilities available under RAD, or request a replacement CHAP to secure RAD rents as may be adjusted in the future.[3]

The PHA confirms its acceptance of the CHAP by submitting an application into the Inventory Removals module in PIC, identifying those units that will be removed from public housing when the RAD conversion is completed.[4] For PBV projects, the PHA is also responsible for confirming that the RAD rents set forth in the CHAP satisfy rent reasonableness requirements.[5]

If a PHA applied for a Portfolio Award, HUD will also reserve RAD conversion authority for the phases or projects covered by the award.[6]

---

1 REV-4 Notice § 1.12.
2 *Id.*
3 *Id.*
4 *Id.*
5 *Id.*
6 *Id.*

The CHAP may be revoked by HUD: (1) if, at any time, the PHA or project become ineligible under the provisions of . . . [the Rev-4 Notice]; (2) upon HUD's determination of financial infeasibility; (3) if the PHA cannot demonstrate to HUD's satisfaction that it is making adequate progress towards Closing; (4) for PHA non-cooperation; (5) for violation of program rules and restrictions, including fraud; (6) if the PHA fails to discuss the conversion plans as a significant action in the PHA's Five-Year Plan, Annual Plan, or MTW Plan or submit an approved significant amendment to HUD; and/or (7) if HUD determines that the terms of the conversion would be inconsistent with fair housing and civil rights laws or a fair housing or civil rights court order, settlement agreement, or voluntary compliance agreement.[7]

Following issuance of the CHAP, the PHA must meet certain milestones related to Financing Plan submission, as further detailed here:[8]

Deadline	Milestone
Thirty (30) days following CHAP issuance	Submit PIC Removal Application.
After CHAP issuance	Hold resident meeting to discuss updated conversion plans and solicit feedback.
After resident meeting	Request Concept Call, in which the PHA describes its conversion plan and demonstrate that the plans are sufficiently developed to warrant review by HUD.
After Concept Call and HUD's invitation for the PHA to submit a Financing Plan	Hold resident meeting to discuss updated conversion plans and the upcoming Financing Plan submission and solicit feedback.

HUD allows a nine-month period (or 270 days) to elapse between CHAP issuance and Financing Plan submission. If the PHA needs additional time to make the Financing Plan submission, HUD may extend the deadline upon the PHA providing a reasonable justification for the delay.[9]

---

7 *Id.* § 1.12(A).
8 *Id.* § 1.12(A)–(C).
9 *Id.* § 1.12(A).

Financing Plan 9

Within sixty (60) days following the Concept Call and HUD's invitation to the PHA to submit a Financing Plan, the PHA must submit the Financing Plan for HUD's review.[1] The Financing Plan submission requirements are fully detailed in Attachment 1A to the RAD Notice.

However, the PHA should allow sufficient time to secure the following long lead items for the Financing Plan:

- Capital Needs Assessment, which informs the RAD scope of work to also be included in the submission;
- Completed environmental review conducted in accordance with 24 C.F.R. Part 50;
- RAD Fair Housing, Accessibility, and Relocation Checklist and any necessary approvals described in the Relocation Notice;
- Proposed financing terms and draft financial models, including construction budget, operating pro forma, including any planned pre-payment of past Capital Fund Financing Program transactions or conversion of a mixed-finance public housing project;
- Market study, if requested by HUD; and
- Approved Significant Amendment to the PHA Plan.[2]

---

1 REV-4 Notice § 1.12(E).

2 *Id*. at Attachment 1A; *see also* REV-4 Notice § 1.15 for a list of applicable requirements for small PHAs.

HUD has the discretion to seek information in addition to those components detailed at Attachment 1A.

For projects involving Federal Housing Administration (FHA)–insured loans, the FHA firm commitment application constitutes the Financing Plan.[3]

The HUD transaction manager assigned to the RAD project will be principally responsible for reviewing the Financing Plan, preparing a transaction memo, which describes the transaction, the key deal points, and confirmation that the transaction complies with various regulatory requirements.

The project's assigned RAD transaction manager will then shepherd the Financing Plan through the review and approval processes. If the project includes an FHA-insured loan, the transaction manager will consult with the HUD Multifamily Hub for the region in which the project is located.[4]

---

3 *Id.* at Attachment 1A.

4 *See* http://www.radresource.net/doc_out.cfm?id=radfhacl for an overview of the closing process for FHA-financed RAD transactions.

RAD Conversion Commitment and Closing Process | 10

Once the Financing Plan is approved, HUD issues the RCC, and the closing process will commence.

The RCC describes the deal specifics set forth in the approved Financing Plan and details the terms and conditions under which HUD will approve the proposed conversion and execute closing documents.[1] It also establishes the legal requirements binding the PHA and, as applicable, the pre-conversion owner (if not the PHA), and the post-conversion owner.[2] For FHA transactions, RCC issuance will be coupled with the issuance of an FHA firm commitment. The form of RCC is nonnegotiable,[3] but it is typically amended ahead of closing to reflect final deal terms.

The PHA and owner(s) must sign and return the fully executed RCC to HUD within thirty (30) days of issuance.[4] The PHA and owner(s) should pay particular attention to any special conditions to closing set forth at Exhibit A to RCC. These conditions must be cleared to HUD's satisfaction in order to close on the transaction.

Per the RCC, closing on the RAD conversion must occur ninety (90) days from the issuance of the RCC, and may be extended by

---

1 REV-4 Notice § 1.13.
2 *Id.* at definition of "RAD Conversion Commitment (RCC)."
3 *Id.*
4 *Id.* § 1.12(D).

HUD.[5] In order to obtain HUD's authorization to close, the PHA must submit a package of draft closing documents to HUD.[6] The closing checklists for both PBV and PBRA transactions are available at the www.radresource. net/doclibrary.cfm site under the "Closing Documents" heading.

Following RCC issuance, a RAD closing coordinator and field counsel will be assigned to review the closing documents. Once all comments provided by the closing coordinator and field counsel are resolved, HUD will execute the release of the public housing Declaration of Trust or Declaration of Restrictive Covenants recorded against the Converting Project, the RAD Use Agreement to be recorded against the Covered Project, and the RAD HAP contract for PBRA projects.[7]

Once the RCC has been issued, but ahead of closing, the PHA must also notify residents that conversion of the project has been approved. This notice must also "address, as appropriate, anticipated timing of the conversion, the anticipated duration of the [scope of work], the revised terms of the lease and house rules, any anticipated relocation, and opportunities and procedures for the exercise of the choice-mobility option."[8]

After the HUD-executed closing documents are delivered to title or an escrow agent, and conditions set forth in HUD's escrow letter are satisfied, the closing on the RAD conversion can occur.[9]

---

5 *Id.* § 1.13.
6 *Id.*
7 *Id.*
8 *Id.* § 1.8(D).
9 *Id.* § 1.13.

Post-Conversion Processing 11

The PHA and RAD project owners have obligations to HUD that continue after RAD conversion.

Most immediately, the parties must submit a partial docket of certain closing documents to HUD within three (3) business days of closing. The full closing docket is due thirty (30) days after closing.[1]

The PHA must also submit the Form-50058 End of Participation for each resident at the Converting Project on or before the last day before the HAP contract's effective date.[2]

The parties must also implement the Choice-Mobility option by the required deadline.[3]

Once the RAD scope of work is completed, the parties must submit a completion certificate to HUD.[4] This certificate includes information about the work, any relocation, and compliance with other RCC requirements, including hiring and labor standards requirements.[5]

In preparation for conversion to permanent financing, the project owner must also submit a certification to HUD.[6] The conversion to permanent financing will be governed by the terms of the loan

---

1 *See* REV-4 Notice § 1.13(A).
2 *Id.* § 1.13(B).
3 *Id.* § 1.6(D)(8) for PBV projects and § 1.7(C)(5) for PBRA projects.
4 *Id.* § 1.13(B)(7).
5 *Id.*
6 *See* Conversion to Permanent Financing—Owner Certification Template on the RAD Resource Desk, www.radresource.net (last visited Feb. 25, 2025).

documents, and generally occurs after occupancy and the cash flow meet a lender-defined standard. If the permanent financing terms have changed from what HUD approved ahead of closing, the project owner may need to submit additional documentation for HUD's approval in order to proceed with conversion.

Prior to submission of the RAD Completion Certificate, most post-closing issues will be handled by the Office of Recapitalization. However, once the RAD Completion Certificate process is complete, post-closing issues will be handled by the Office of Public Housing Investments for PBV projects and the Office of Housing for PBRA projects.

For more detail about common post-closing issues and how they should be addressed with HUD, please see HUD's latest Post-Conversion Processing Guide on the RAD Resource Desk.[7]

---

7 RAD Resource Desk, www.radresource.net/pha_data2020.cfm (last visited Feb. 25, 2025).

RAD/Section 18 Blend

12

The opportunity to blend RAD with Section 18 (RAD/Section 18 Blend) serves as a preservation tool that can make the conversion of public housing under RAD more financially feasible by awarding tenant protection vouchers (TPV) at higher Section 8 rents for a portion of the Converting Project's units.[1]

The program blends the benefits of the RAD program, such as the use of public housing funds to support the conversion and the application of the RAD resident protections, with the benefits of a Section 18 disposition,[2] namely higher contract rents, which can then support additional financing and higher levels of physical repair for the Covered Project.

There are two types of projects eligible for the RAD/Section 18 Blend: the construction blend, which determines the number of TPVs based on the level of construction or rehabilitation in the project (Construction Blend),[3] and a project owned by a small PHA[4] that intends to close out its public housing program (Small PHA Blend).

---

1 *See* Notice PIH 2021-07 (HA), issued January 19, 2021 (RAD/S18 Blend Notice), at Section 3(A)(2)(e) and Notice H-2023-08 PIH 2023-19 (HA), issued July 27, 2023 (Supplemental RAD Notice 4B).

2 42 U.S.C. 1437p. Section 18 sets forth the process by which a PHA may demolish or dispose of public housing property.

3 The Construction Blend is not available to projects using nine percent (9%) Low Income Housing Tax Credits. *See* Section 3(A)(2)(e)(1) of the RAD/S18 Blend Notice.

4 A small PHA has 250 or fewer public housing units. See Section 3(A)(2)(e)(2) of the RAD/S18 Blend Notice.

A Small PHA Blend does not require that the PHA close out its public housing program through the RAD transaction, but the PHA must submit to HUD a feasible repositioning plan to close out its entire public housing program.[5]

The RAD/Section 18 Blend builds off the success of previous blend programs by simplifying the point of contact, which allows for a streamlined process. Similar to RAD applications, RAD/Section 18 Blends are primarily processed by the Office of Recapitalization. For the sake of continuity, RAD/Section 18 Blends are subject to the RAD requirements and processes in all aspects, including the Financing Plan, underwriting, the release of the Declaration of Trust, treatment of proceeds in the disposition, relocation and resident rights requirements, and placement of a long-term use agreement at the Covered Project.[6] Projects using the RAD/Section 18 Blend must also still meet the RAD program's "substantial conversion of assistance" requirements.[7]

Commencing at the RAD conversion closing, the Covered Project will receive rental subsidy through a single HAP contract.[8] The RAD HAP contract will include "a single, blended rent schedule for all units resulting from a RAD/Section 18 Blend," which will be calculated as the unit-weighted average contract rent by bedroom of:

- the RAD rents generated for the percentage of RAD units based on the public housing Operating Funds and Capital Funds allocated to the units pre-conversion; and
- the funds generated by tenant protection voucher assistance for the applicable percentage of Section 18 units in the Covered Project.

---

5 *Id. See* Notice PIH 2016-23 (HA), issued December 7, 2026, for more information about HUD's closeout requirements.

6 *Id.*

7 *Id.* at Section 3(A)(2)(e).

8 Note that the FY 2024 Act authorizes the use of a single HAP contract for the RAD units and the Section 18 units in RAD/Section 18 Blend transactions. However, as of the publication date of this Guide, HUD has not yet issued guidance to implement this change.

Similar to the units in a RAD-only project, the project units in a RAD/
Section 18 Blend (both RAD and non-RAD PBV units resulting from the
RAD/Section 18 Blend) are exempt from certain PBV requirements under
24 C.F.R. Part 983, such as competitive selection, the project cap, and the
program cap.[9]

---

9 *See* Supplemental RAD Notice 4B and the flexibilities provided to former public housing
projects undergoing redevelopment under the Housing Opportunity through Modernization
Act of 2016, as implemented by Notice PIH 2017-21.

Restore–Rebuild **13**

In 1998, Congress amended the Housing Act[1] to limit the construction and operation of new public housing units funded with Capital Funds or Operating Funds if the construction of those units would result in a net increase in the number of units the PHA owned, assisted, or operated as of October 1, 1999 (Faircloth Limit).[2] A PHA's Faircloth Limit is adjusted when a PHA removes units from, adds units to, or consolidates units under the PHA's the Annual Contributions Contract, including removals due to RAD conversions.

Currently, the public housing program is operating approximately 260,000 units below the Faircloth Limit.[3] The difference between a PHA's Faircloth Limit and the number of units it currently operates is known as its "Faircloth Authority."[4] The available Faircloth Authority is disbursed among PHAs nationwide, with many PHAs holding authority to create more than 1,000 units before hitting their Faircloth Limit.[5]

---

1 Section 9(g)(3) of the Housing Act.
2 *Id.*
3 National List of Maximum Number of Units Eligible for Capital Funding and Operating Subsidy by PHA as of October 15, 2023, https://www.hud.gov/program_offices/public_indian_housing/programs/ph/capfund (last visited Feb. 25, 2024).
4 *See* Restore–Rebuild Guide, Nov. 2024, https://www.hud.gov/sites/dfiles/Housing/documents/Restore-Rebuild_Guide_11-2024.pdf.
5 *Id.*

HUD created the Restore–Rebuild (formerly referred to as "Faircloth-to-RAD") conversions to enable PHAs to use their Faircloth Authority to produce new public housing units through acquisition, rehabilitation, or new construction, with a conditional pre-approval from HUD to convert the units to long-term Section 8 under the RAD program after the units qualify as public housing units.[6]

The new units are initially developed under HUD's mixed-finance program. Mixed-finance development requires ownership of the public housing units by an entity other than the PHA and financing from multiple sources, which can be public and private sources.[7]

Once the units are constructed in accordance with the mixed-finance requirements, and the requisite construction completion documentation is submitted to and accepted by HUD's Office of Recapitalization, the Actual Date of Full Availability can be determined, and the units can be added to PIC.[8]

After the units are entered into PIC, HUD's Office of Recapitalization will issue the CHAP and then the RCC. The issuance of the RCC will allow the PHA to proceed with the RAD conversion process, and a RAD closing coordinator and field counsel will be assigned. Similar to a traditional RAD conversion, HUD requires PHAs to comply with all resident notice requirements under the RAD program, which may vary depending on when the residents occupy the Covered Project.[9]

Please find here a timeline for the development of new units using the Restore–Rebuild process.

[Insert timeline from the middle of page 6 of the Restore-Rebuild guidance at https://www.hud.gov/sites/dfiles/Housing/documents/ Restore-Rebuild_Guide_11–2024.pdf]

HUD's Office of Public Housing Investments oversees the development of the units under the mixed-finance requirements. However, the Office of

---

6 *Id.*
7 *See* 24 C.F.R. 905, subpt. F.
8 Restore-Rebuild Guide, *supra* note 4.
9 *Id.*

Recapitalization is also involved throughout the development process in preparation for the eventual RAD conversion. The two offices work together to streamline the mixed-finance development and RAD conversion processes and avoid duplication of efforts through the life cycle of these transactions.[10]

10 *Id.*

Conclusion

The Rental Assistance Demonstration has come a long way in its first decade, as it has become a valuable tool used to tackle the overwhelming public housing capital needs backlog. RAD has been utilized by thousands of projects in 48 states plus the District of Columbia, Puerto Rico, and the U.S. Virgin Islands. These units have been preserved as affordable with long-term public subsidy and access to private capital.

RAD has shown to be an efficient and effective process to transfer subsidy from the public housing platform to the Section 8 platform. Even as RAD continues to be a demonstration, it has become a mainstream preservation option for PHAs that want to use it.

RAD has evolved through multiple implementation and supplemental notices, and it continues to change in order to maximize the regulatory and statutory flexibility afforded to the demonstration through the RAD statutory authority.

RAD has required PHAs, HUD, private developers, lenders, and investors to work together to innovate funding and operations of affordable housing. The need for preserving existing public housing and the need to increase affordable housing are not diminishing, and RAD's innovation and evolution will continue into its second decade and beyond to meet these needs.

About the Authors

Amy M. McClain is a partner at Ballard Spahr LLP and chair of the firm's Real Estate Department. Courtney E. Hunter is Of Counsel at Ballard Spahr. Their work includes representation of affordable housing developers and housing authorities in the revitalization of many of the nation's low-income communities, addressing statutory and regulatory concerns along with complex real estate development and finance matters. They greatly appreciate the assistance of several individuals providing feedback regarding the draft, including Kathryn Oates with Regional Housing Legal Services; Georgi Banna and Sumbul Alam, both formerly at Ballard Spahr; and Mary Grace Folwell and Sireen Tucker with Ballard Spahr.

Index

accessibility requirements, 24
Annual Contributions Contract, 53
application submission, 13–17, 39
asset repositioning fees, 21

Capital Fund Financing Program, 19, 43
Capital Funds, 2, 6, 19–20, 50, 53
Capital Needs Assessment (CNA), 5, 43
CHAP. *See* Commitment to Enter into a Housing Assistance Payment (CHAP)
Choice-Mobility commitment letter, 15
Choice-Mobility requirement, 7, 15
climate resilience, 23
CNA. *See* Capital Needs Assessment (CNA)
Commitment to Enter into a Housing Assistance Payment (CHAP), 3, 5, 11, 13–14, 17, 22, 34, 39, 41–42, 54
Concept Call, 11, 42–43

Consolidated and Further Continuing Appropriations Act of 2012, 1
Covered Project, 3, 28–29, 33, 39, 46, 49–50, 54

Davis-Bacon requirements, 25
DDTF. *See* Demolition and Disposition Transitional Funding (DDTF)
Declaration of Trust, 3, 46, 50
demolition, 20, 22, 34, 39
Demolition and Disposition Transitional Funding (DDTF), 21
disposition, 20–22, 49–50

energy-efficiency standards, 23
Energy Independence Act of 2007, 23

Faircloth Authority, 53–54
Faircloth Limit, 22, 53
Fair Housing, Accessibility, and Relocation Checklist, 43
Fair Housing and Equal Opportunity (FHEO), 30, 38

Family Self-Sufficiency (FSS), 22, 29
feasibility analysis, 5–7
Federal Housing Administration
(FHA), 44–45
FHA. *See* Federal Housing
Administration (FHA)
FHEO. *See* Fair Housing and
Equal Opportunity (FHEO)
financing, 15–17, 26, 28, 33,
47–49, 54
Financing Plan, 3, 5, 7, 11, 15,
19, 23, 25, 28, 38–39, 42–45, 50
FSS. *See* Family Self-Sufficiency (FSS)

General Information Notice (GIN),
34–35, 39
GIN. *See* General Information
Notice (GIN)
green building, 23

HAP. *See* Housing Assistance
Payments (HAP)
Housing Act of 1937, 2, 7, 22,
27–28, 53
Housing Assistance Payments
(HAP), 2–3, 6–7, 15–16, 20,
25–26, 41, 46–47, 50
Housing Opportunity Through
Modernization Act, 7

initiation of negotiations (ION),
32, 35–36, 39
insurance, mandatory, 26
ION. *See* initiation of negotiations
(ION)

mixed-finance affidavit,
14–15
monitoring requirements, 25
Moving to Work (MTW), 16,
23, 42
MTW. *See* Moving to Work
(MTW)

neighborhood standards, 24
NOIA. *See* Notice of Intent to
Acquire (NOIA)
Notice of Intent to Acquire
(NOIA), 36, 39

OCAF. *See* operating cost
adjustment factor (OCAF)
operating cost adjustment factor
(OCAF), 2, 6
Operating Funds, 2, 6, 19–20, 53

PBRA. *See* project-based rental
assistance (PBRA)
PBV. *See* project-based vouchers
(PBV)
PHAS. *See* Public Housing
Assessment System (PHAS)
planning, 5, 38–39
portfolio applications, 16–17
Portfolio Award Letter, 14, 17
post-conversion processing,
47–48
Program Sunset Date, 3–4, 13–14
project-based rental assistance
(PBRA), 1, 5–7, 10, 15–16,
24–25, 27–28, 46, 48

project-based vouchers (PBV), 1,
5–7, 10, 16, 25, 27–28, 41, 46,
48, 51
Public Housing Assessment System
(PHAS), 22

RAD. *See* Rental Assistance
Demonstration (RAD)
RAD Completion Certificate, 48
RAD Conversion Commitment
(RCC), 3, 11–12, 19, 25, 32, 35,
39, 45–47, 54
RAD Information Notice (RIN),
9–10, 32, 39
RAD Notice, 4, 10, 15–16, 19–20,
22–29, 37, 43
RAD Notice of Relocation, 35–36
RCC. *See* RAD Conversion
Commitment (RCC)
records access, 24
refinancing, future, 26
regulatory waivers, 19–26
relocation, 9, 24, 27, 29–39
Relocation and Accessibility
Checklist, 30, 38
relocation assistance, 30–32, 34,
36–37
Relocation Notice, 27, 30, 32–37,
39, 43
Rental Assistance Demonstration
(RAD):57; application
submission, 13–17; approval,
41; closing process, 45–46;
conversion process, 2–4;
feasibility analysis, 5–7;

financing, 43–44; goals of, 1;
post-conversion processing,
47–48; precursors to, 1;
relocation, 31–39; residents,
9–12, 27–38; Restore-Rebuild
conversions, 53–55; Section 18
Blend, 49–51; statutory and
regulatory waivers, 19–26
rents, bundled, 15–16
Replacement Housing Factor
(RHF), 20–21
rescreening, of residents upon
conversion, 27–28, 33
resident(s): engagement, 9–12;
notice, 31–32; notification of,
32–38; participation, 28–29;
protections, 27–30; rescreening
of, 27–28; right to return,
29–30
Resident Opportunities and Self-
Sufficiency Service Coordinators
(ROSS), 22, 29
Restore-Rebuild, 53–55
RHF. *See* Replacement Housing
Factor (RHF)
right to return, 29–30
RIN. *See* RAD Information Notice
(RIN)
ROSS. *See* Resident Opportunities
and Self-Sufficiency
Service Coordinators (ROSS)

Section 3, 25
Section 8, 1–2, 4, 6–7, 10, 15, 49,
54, 57

Section 9, 2
Section 18, 20–21, 49–51
Section 23, 22
Section 33 Conversion Review, 22
Section 34, 22
site selection, 24
statutory waivers, 19–26
sunset date, 3–4, 13–14

TBV. *See* tenant-based Housing
    Choice Voucher (TBV)
tenant-based Housing Choice
    Voucher (TBV), 7, 15

tenant protection voucher
    (TPV), 49
TPV. *See* tenant protection voucher
    (TPV)
Transforming Rental Assistance, 1

Uniform Relocation Act (URA), 9,
    24, 27, 30, 32–39
Unit Cap, 3–4, 13
URA. *See* Uniform Relocation Act
    (URA)

waiting lists, 13, 25–26